*kindness*

## Other Studies in the Fruit of the Spirit Bible Study Series

# kindness

## Reaching Out to Others
### Phyllis J. Le Peau

GRAND RAPIDS, MICHIGAN 49530

# ZONDERVAN™

*Kindness: Reaching Out to Others*
Copyright © 1991, 2001 by Phyllis J. Le Peau
Requests for information should be addressed to:
Zondervan, *Grand Rapids, Michigan 49530*

ISBN 0-310-23866-8

Study 6 is adapted from a study in *Caring for Physical Needs* in the Caring People Series from InterVarsity Press and is used by permission.

*Interior design by Melissa Elenbaas*

*Printed in the United States of America*

10 11 12 /❖ CH/ 15 14 13 12 11 10 9

# CONTENTS

# FRUIT OF THE SPIRIT
## BIBLE STUDIES

Welcome to Fruit of the Spirit Bible Studies. This series was written with one goal in mind—to allow the Spirit of God to use the Word of God to produce his fruit in your life.

To get the most from this series you need to understand a few basic facts:

Fruit of the Spirit Bible Studies are designed to be flexible. You can use them in your quiet times or for group discussion. They are ideal for Sunday school classes, small groups, or neighborhood Bible studies.

The eight guides in this series can be used in any order that is best for you or your group.

Because each guide contains only six studies, you can easily explore more than one fruit of the Spirit. In a Sunday school class, any two guides can be combined for a quarter (twelve weeks), or the entire series can be covered in a year.

Each study deliberately focuses on only one or two passages. That allows you to see each passage in its context, avoiding the temptation of prooftexting and the frustration of "Bible hopscotch" (jumping from verse to verse). If you would like to look up additional passages, a Bible concordance will give the most help.

The questions help you *discover* what the Bible says rather than simply *telling* you what it says. They encourage you to think and to explore options rather than to merely fill in the blanks with one-word answers.

Leader's notes are provided in the back of the guide. They show how to lead a group discussion, provide additional information on questions, and suggest ways to deal with problems that may come up in the discussion. With such helps, someone with little or no experience can lead an effective study.

## SUGGESTIONS FOR INDIVIDUAL STUDY

1. Begin each study with prayer. Ask God to help you understand the passage and to apply it to your life.

2. A good modern translation, such as the *New International Version,* the *New American Standard Bible,* or the *Revised Standard Version,* will give you the most help. However, the questions in this guide are based on the *New International Version.*

3. Read and reread the passage(s). You must know what the passage says before you can understand what it means and how it applies to you.

4. Write your answers in the space provided in the study guide. This will help you to clearly express your understanding of the passage.

5. Keep a Bible dictionary handy. Use it to look up any unfamiliar words, names, or places.

## SUGGESTIONS FOR GROUP STUDY

1. Come to the study prepared. Careful preparation will greatly enrich your time in group discussion.

2. Be willing to join in the discussion. The leader of the group will not be lecturing but will encourage people to discuss what they have learned in the passage. Plan to share what God has taught you in your individual study.

3. Stick to the passage being studied. Base your answers on the verses being discussed rather than on outside authorities such as commentaries or your favorite author or speaker.

4. Try to be sensitive to the other members of the group. Listen attentively when they speak, and be affirming whenever you can. This will encourage more hesitant members of the group to participate.

5. Be careful not to dominate the discussion. By all means, participate! But allow others to have equal time.

6. If you are the discussion leader, you will find additional suggestions and helpful ideas in the leader's notes at the back of the guide.

# KINDNESS

## Reaching Out to Others

Several years ago some seminary students were asked to preach on the story of the good Samaritan. When the hour arrived for their sermon, each one was deliberately delayed en route to class. As the students raced across campus, they encountered a person who pretended to be in need. Ironically, not one of the students stopped to help. After all, they had an important sermon to preach!

It's easy to laugh at the hypocrisy of those students. Yet every day in various ways we reenact Christ's parable. Whether it's a family on the side of the road with car trouble, a homeless person sleeping over an outdoor heating vent, or a panhandler asking for spare change—we either pass by or reach out in kindness.

These daily opportunities make me excited about exploring what the Bible says about kindness and goodness. (The two words/concepts are very close in both Hebrew and Greek, so we will consider them together in this guide.)

What we discover is that the word for kindness is much richer in meaning than its English translation would suggest. The NIV translates the Hebrew word *hesed* as "kindness" (41 times), "love" (129 times), "unfailing love" (32 times), "unfailing kindness" (3 times), and "loving-kindness" (1 time). The Hebrew lexicon suggests that it can also be translated as "goodness." The Greek word is also rich and diverse in meaning. The word is broad because the kindness and love of God are broad, reaching out to those in need.

The Bible tells us that God's kindness is freely given, that it preserves us, and that it is "better than life." It involves the warmth of God's fellowship as well as the security of his goodness and faithfulness.

It certainly follows that if we experience God's kindness, we will be transformed by it and reach out in kindness to others. It is with this hope that we begin to explore this multifaceted fruit of the Spirit.

This guide includes six studies for groups or individuals. Four look at principles of kindness and goodness: God's kindness to us, showing kindness to others, fulfilling the law of Christ, and reaching out to the poor and needy. Because kindness is seen most clearly in real life, we will also look at two examples of kindness in the relationships between Ruth and Boaz, and David and Mephibosheth.

As you reflect on each passage of Scripture, may you experience the Lord's kindness, be transformed by it, and demonstrate it to others.

o n e

# GOD'S KINDNESS TO US

*Psalm 103*

There are a lot of parallels between being children in a physical sense and being a child of God. One of the most blatant similarities is gratefulness—or the lack thereof. Children are often self-centered and at times are hardly aware of the kindness that is extended to them by their parents.

As God's children, our awareness and appreciation of his kindness should be as natural as breathing fresh air. Yet that is not always the case. We need eyes that see and hearts that believe that God's kindness extends to us. As you look closely at God's kindness in Psalm 103, ask him to open your eyes to all that is there.

## Warming Up

1. What do you think it would be like never to have experienced God's kindness?

## Digging In

2.     Read Psalm 103. According to verses 2–5, what kind and loving things has God done for us?

3.     In this first paragraph (vv. 2–5), how does God's loving-kindness meet our physical, emotional, and spiritual needs?

4.     Which of the Lord's "benefits" have you experienced this week? Explain.

5.    As you read the psalmist's description of God in verses 6–14, what
      kind of portrait emerges?

6.    How are God's kindness and love demonstrated in his treatment
      of the oppressed (vv. 6–7)?

7.    How is God's loving-kindness revealed in the way he treats those
      who sin (vv. 8–12)?

8. In what ways do you struggle with accepting God's forgiveness?

How can these verses help you to live in the freedom of his forgiveness?

9. How does God respond to our frailty and mortality (vv. 13–19)?

10. How do his compassion and love reach even beyond the grave for those who fear him?

11. Reflect again on the ways God's loving-kindness has been shown to you according to this psalm. In what specific ways could you imitate his kindness in your relationships with others?

## *Pray about It*

Praise to God is an appropriate way to open and close this psalm. Using verses 1–2 and 20–22 as your model, pray to God, praising him for his kindness, love, and compassion. Ask him to produce in you the fruit of kindness.

## TAKING THE NEXT STEP

Often in our prayer life, praise is short-lived. We move quickly to requests both for ourselves and others. The people of Israel quickly forgot who God was and what he had done for them.

"Blessing (praising) God combines the bowing of the knee in reverence for his holy name, and opening the heart in adoring gratitude for all his benefits. Upon this task the psalmist focuses his essential self, or soul, and unites all his individual faculties" (*The New Bible Commentary: Revised* [Grand Rapids, Mich.: Eerdmans, 1970], 515).

Using Psalm 104 as a model, take several days to pray a prayer of praise to God. (You might want to write this prayer out.) First praise him for every detail that you see in this psalm about who God is. Then praise him for his kind works. Finally, praise him for how you have been touched by who he is and what he has done.

two

# SHOWING KINDNESS TO OTHERS

*Matthew 10:40–42; Mark 9:33–37*

According to Greek mythology, the god Jupiter decided to find out how hospitable the people of Phrygia were. He and his companion, Mercury, dressed as poor wayfarers and wandered from door to door, asking for food and a place to rest. At every house they were treated rudely, and doors were slammed in their faces.

At last they came to the poorest hovel and were greeted by a kindly faced old man named Philemon and his wife, Baucis. The couple welcomed them warmly and invited them in. They gave them seats by the fire and hurried to make them a meal. Although the couple had only diluted wine to offer, they eagerly refilled their guest's cups as soon as they were empty.

Because of the couple's generous hospitality, Jupiter rewarded them richly. Their container of wine never ran dry, and their home was transformed into a temple, over which they were appointed as priests and guardians.

Although the story is myth, the principle it teaches is quite biblical: We should never underestimate the worth of our guests or the value of any act of kindness.

1.    Are you ever tempted to treat some people better than others? Why?

## Digging In

2.    Read Matthew 10:40–42. What various types of people does Christ view as his representatives?

What motivation are we given for "receiving" each one?

3.    How would you respond if Christ himself came to your home, asking for food, shelter, or clothing?

4.    How does it help you to know that by showing kindness to the least of Christ's followers, you are showing kindness to Jesus and his Father?

5.    Jesus mentions the word *reward* three times in three verses. What type of reward do you imagine you will receive for showing kindness to other Christians?

Does the promise of a reward give you any additional motivation? Why or why not?

6.    Read Mark 9:33–37. Why do you suppose the disciples were arguing about who was the greatest?

7.    What are some of the marks and symbols of greatness in our culture?

8.  How does Jesus stand the world's concept of greatness on its head (v. 35)?

9.  In what practical ways might you be "the very last, and the servant of all" at home and in your church?

10. Children had a lowly place in Jewish society (v. 36). What types of people are we inclined to view as lowly in our culture?

11.    In what sense does Christ's statement (v. 37) obliterate such distinctions?

12.    Think of one person you know who might be viewed as lowly by others. In what specific ways might you treat that person with kindness by receiving, welcoming, or giving a cup of cold water to that person for Christ's sake?

## Pray about It

Make a list of every Christian you know who might be perceived as lowly by those in our culture (e.g., missionaries). Pray for them daily for the next week.

## TAKING THE NEXT STEP

In order to live a life of radical kindness in this world as representatives of Jesus, we must first relinquish the right to our own life. We "must be the very last, and the servant of all" (Mark 9:35). Write a paraphrase in your own words on the following passages that have to do with this radical lifestyle: Matthew 10:37–39; John 13:1–17; Philippians 2:1–11.

Ask God to build the fruit of kindness into you by integrating the truth of these passages into your life.

three

# KINDNESS ILLUSTRATED: BOAZ AND RUTH

## *Ruth 2*

The events in the book of Ruth are set in the time of the judges. That period spanned the first two or three centuries after Israel entered Canaan under Joshua's leadership. Because of a famine in Bethlehem, a man named Elimelech, his wife, Naomi, and their two sons migrated to the country of Moab. In the ten years that they lived there, the two sons married Moabite women, and then the two sons and their father died. Left alone and destitute, Naomi heard that the Lord had provided food in Judah. Naomi's daughter-in-law Ruth was willing to leave her family, homeland, and all that was comfortable to her because of her love and loyalty to Naomi. Together they traveled to Bethlehem.

Our study begins in chapter 2, where Ruth, though a foreigner in a strange land, is shown great kindness.

## Warming Up

1.   Have you ever received kindness from a total stranger? How were you affected by that act of kindness?

## Digging In

2.     Read Ruth 2. Ruth's commitment to Naomi was so great that she left all to go with her to a strange land. How does Ruth continue to demonstrate her loyalty?

3.     How do Ruth and Boaz meet?

4.     Look closely at Boaz. What do you learn about him in verses 4–16?

5.    Why does Boaz respond to Ruth in such a kind way (vv. 10–12)?

      How does Boaz describe the Lord to Ruth (v. 12)?

6.    What specific needs of Ruth does Boaz meet?

7.    How is Ruth affected by Boaz's kindness?

How would you have been affected?

8.    What do you think it means that Ruth received "comfort" (v. 13) because of his kindness?

9.   When have you been comforted by someone's kindness?

10.  In verses 19–22, what is Naomi's response to Boaz's kindness?

11.  How is the rippling (multiplying) effect of kindness illustrated throughout this passage?

12.   Think of someone in your family who needs to experience God's kindness through you. What are the first steps you need to take to show kindness to that person?

## *Pray about It*

Ask God to allow the fruit of kindness to grow freely in you and to be demonstrated this week, especially in your family.

---

### TAKING THE NEXT STEP

Often it is most difficult to express kindness to members of our family or to those with whom we closely live. Make a kindness plan for the people within your household. Plan one act of kindness a day. Record both their response and how you felt about it.

four

# FULFILLING THE LAW OF CHRIST

*Galatians 6:1–10*

In Truman Capote's *Other Voices, Other Rooms,* the hero is about to walk along a heavy but rotting beam over a brooding, murky creek. Starting over, "stepping gingerly . . . he felt he would never reach the other side: always he would be balanced here, suspended between land and in the dark and alone. Then feeling the board shake as Idabel started across, he remembered that he had someone to be together with. And he could go on."[1]

Having someone with us during hard times can make the difference between going on and giving up. In Galatians 6 Paul urges us to fulfill the law of Christ by carrying each other's burdens.

## Warming Up

1.  Think of your closest friend. In what ways has he or she made life's burdens easier to bear?

---

1 As quoted by Maxie D. Dunnam, *Galatians, Ephesians, Philippians, Colossians, Philemon,* The Communicator's Commentary (Waco, Tex.: Word, 1982), 122.

## Digging In

2.      Read Galatians 6:1–10. What instructions does Paul give concerning someone who is caught in a sin?

         How would you feel if you were "caught in a sin" by members of your church?

3.      Why is gentleness extremely important in the response to someone caught in sin?

4. Paul urges us to "carry each other's burdens" (v. 2). What types of burdens often press down or even crush you and/or people around you?

5. In what specific ways might you make their burden lighter? How could someone else help make your burdens lighter?

6. In what sense do we "fulfill the law of Christ" (v. 2) by carrying each other's burdens?

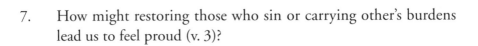

7.    How might restoring those who sin or carrying other's burdens lead us to feel proud (v. 3)?

8.    What does Paul say we should do to avoid this pitfall (vv. 4–5)?

9.    What do you think is involved in testing your own actions?

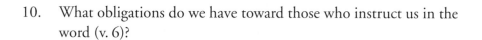
10. What obligations do we have toward those who instruct us in the word (v. 6)?

What kinds of "good things" do you think Paul has in mind?

11. At first, it seems that Paul's warnings about sowing and reaping come out of nowhere (vv. 7–9). How does his analogy relate to doing good to others?

12.   Why might we become weary and be tempted to give up as we express kindness to those in need (vv. 7–9)?

13.   Give one specific example of how you might live out the fruit of kindness in the life of a Christian or non-Christian that you know.

## Pray about It

Thank God for the community of believers in which he has placed you. Pray that the Holy Spirit will make you aware of specific ways that you can express the fruit of kindness to people within your community.

## TAKING THE NEXT STEP

Write a letter of encouragement and affirmation to your pastor this week. Include such things as your appreciation for his/her study of the Scriptures, teaching, faithful service to the congregation, character, integrity, and love for the Lord.

five

# REACHING OUT TO THE POOR AND NEEDY

*Proverbs 14:21, 31; 19:17*

Hudson Taylor, famous missionary to China and founder of the China Inland Mission, was called to a home to pray for a sick woman. He was called because, unlike other religious leaders of the day, he did not charge the family to pray for her.

The woman was very poor. When Taylor saw her poverty, he clutched the coin in his pocket. It was the only money he had. He wished that there were two so he could give one to her. After all, he could not give her his only coin! What would he do to survive? He had only two meals left at home for himself.

He knelt to pray for the woman but found that he could not pray. God was asking him to give up his precious coin. He tried again to pray. How could he walk away with nothing to live on? Again, he could not pray. Finally, he gave her the coin. He was released by God and felt great freedom and blessing as he prayed.

Hudson Taylor's experience provides one example of what it means to reach out to the poor and needy—something God asks from us even when we are poor and needy ourselves.

1.    Who are some of the poor and needy that live in your area?

## Digging In

2.    Read Proverbs 14:21. Do you tend to view the needy as your neighbors? Why or why not?

3.    What acts of kindness might we show to those in need?

4.    How have you felt God's blessing as a result of being kind to the needy?

5.    Read Proverbs 14:31. In what ways are the poor oppressed in our society?

Why do you think so many have so little materially, while a few have so much?

6.     When have you oppressed the poor, either directly or indirectly?

7.     "Shows contempt for their Maker" are strong words. Why do you think oppressing the poor shows contempt for God?

8.     Conversely, how does being kind to the needy honor God?

9.  Read Proverbs 19:17. In what sense are we loaning to the Lord when we are kind to the poor?

10. Do you think our "reward" is something we will receive now, in the future, or both? Explain.

11. What do these proverbs reveal about God's concern for the poor?

What actions and attitudes toward the poor do you think God expects from us?

12. What specific ways can you honor God this week by being kind to the poor and needy?

## Pray about It

Confess your sin of oppressing the poor. Ask the Lord to reveal to you any ways that you oppress the poor that you may not be aware of. Thank him for his love for the poor and needy and for his forgiveness to you.

---

### TAKING THE NEXT STEP

Investigate opportunities for serving the poor through a soup kitchen, food pantry, or homeless shelter. Volunteer to serve at one of these places for an afternoon.

---

# KINDNESS ILLUSTRATED: DAVID AND MEPHIBOSHETH

*2 Samuel 9*

We have very special friends coming to live with us this summer. We are excited about the time we will have with them. We are also anticipating a great time with their three sons, though we have never met them. Because we love Jackie and Steve, we love Jeremy, Chris, and Justin and have already decided to embrace them as our own children. Because of our love and loyalty for their parents, the boys have a place in our hearts.

So it was with David. Because of David's deep love for Jonathan, David went out of his way to show kindness to Jonathan's son Mephibosheth.

## Warming Up

1. When have you shown kindness to someone you did not know? Why?

## Digging In

2.  What do you know about David and Jonathan's relationship?
    (Glance through 1 Samuel 18:1–4; 19:1–5; and 20:1–23 for more
    information.)

    How would you describe their love and loyalty to each other?

3.  Read 2 Samuel 9. What steps did David go through to find
    Mephibosheth (vv. 1–5)?

4.    What motivated David to find him and show kindness to him?

5.    How does your love and loyalty for a person motivate you to show
      kindness to his or her relatives?

6.    How would you describe Mephibosheth?

Why would he be an unlikely candidate to receive kindness from David?

7.   How extensive were the needs that David met?

8.   Verse 3 states that David wanted to show *God's* kindness. How is David's kindness to Mephibosheth like God's kindness to us?

9.      Describe a situation in which you experienced God's kindness
        through a person you did not know. How were you affected?

10.     David took risks in showing kindness to Mephibosheth. His king-
        dom could have been threatened by allowing someone from the
        previous dynasty to live. What risks do we take when we express
        kindness to people?

## Pray about It

Think of someone who needs to experience God's kindness through you.
Ask God to give you opportunities to express his kindness to that person.

## TAKING THE NEXT STEP

Think about a friend who is a single parent or one who has an elderly parent who is lonely. Show God's kindness to that person by doing such things as helping with child care, visiting, calling, writing a note of encouragement, fixing a meal, or bringing in groceries.

# LEADER'S NOTES

Leading a Bible discussion—especially for the first time— can make you feel both nervous and excited. If you are nervous, realize that you are in good company. Many biblical leaders, such as Moses, Joshua, and the apostle Paul, felt nervous and inadequate to lead others (see, for example, 1 Cor. 2:3). Yet God's grace was sufficient for them, just as it will be for you.

Some excitement is also natural. Your leadership is a gift to the others in the group. Keep in mind, however, that other group members also share responsibility for the group. Your role is simply to stimulate discussion by asking questions and encouraging people to respond. The suggestions listed below can help you to be an effective leader.

## PREPARING TO LEAD

1. Ask God to help you understand and apply the passage to your own life. Unless that happens, you will not be prepared to lead others.
2. Carefully work through each question in the study guide. Meditate and reflect on the passage as you formulate your answers.
3. Familiarize yourself with the leader's notes for the study. These will help you understand the purpose of the study and will provide valuable information about the questions in the study.
4. Pray for the various members of the group. Ask God to use these studies to bring about greater spiritual fruit in the life of each person.

5. Before the first meeting, make sure each person has a study guide. Encourage them to prepare beforehand for each study.

## LEADING THE STUDY

1. Begin the study on time. If people realize that the study begins on schedule, they will work harder to arrive on time.

2. At the beginning of your first time together, explain that these studies are designed to be discussions not lectures. Encourage everyone to participate, but realize that some may be hesitant to speak during the first few sessions.

3. Read the introductory paragraph at the beginning of the discussion. This will orient the group to the passage being studied.

4. Read the passage aloud. You may choose to do this yourself, or you might ask for volunteers.

5. The questions in the guide are designed to be used just as they are written. If you wish, you may simply read each one aloud to the group. Or you may prefer to express them in your own words. However, unnecessary rewording of the questions is not recommended.

6. Don't be afraid of silence. People in the group may need time to think before responding.

7. Avoid answering your own questions. If necessary, rephrase a question until it is clearly understood. Even an eager group will quickly become passive and silent if they think the leader will do most of the talking.

8. Encourage more than one answer to each question. Ask, "What do the rest of you think?" or "Anyone else?" until several people have had a chance to respond.

9. Try to be affirming whenever possible. Let people know you appreciate their insights into the passage.

10. Never reject an answer. If it is clearly wrong, ask, "Which verse led you to that conclusion?" Or let the group handle the problem by asking them what they think about the question.

11. Avoid going off on tangents. If people wander off course, gently bring them back to the passage being considered.

12. Conclude your time together with conversational prayer. Ask God to help you apply those things that you learned in the study.

13. End on time. This will be easier if you control the pace of the discussion by not spending too much time on some questions or too little on others.

Many more suggestions and helps are found in the book *Leading Bible Discussions* (InterVarsity). Reading that would be well worth your time.

*Study 1*

## GOD'S KINDNESS TO US

*Psalm 103*

**Purpose:** To reflect on and respond to God's wonderful kindness.

"The psalm is an expression of praise evoked firstly by the psalmist's own experience (note the singular pronouns in vv. 1–5). But it is tremendously strengthened by the evidences of the Lord's amazing compassion and mercy toward men in general: His forgiveness and solicitude for such insignificant creatures as men must lead to universal adoration" (*The New Bible Commentary: Revised* [Grand Rapids, Mich.: Eerdmans, 1970], 515).

**Question 1.** Every study begins with an "approach question," which is discussed *before* reading the passage. An approach question is designed to do three things.

First, it helps to break the ice. Because an approach question doesn't require any knowledge of the passage or any special preparation, it can get people talking and can help them to warm up to each other.

Second, an approach question can motivate people to study the passage at hand. At the beginning of the study, people in the group aren't necessarily ready to jump into the world of the Bible. Their minds may be on other things (their kids, a problem at work, an upcoming meeting) that have nothing to do with the study. An approach question can capture their interest and draw them into the discussion by raising important issues related to the study. The question becomes a bridge between their personal lives and the answers found in Scripture.

Third, a good approach question can reveal where people's thoughts or feelings need to be transformed by Scripture. That is why it is important to ask the approach question *before* reading the passage. The passage might inhibit the spontaneous, honest answers people might have given, because they feel compelled to give biblical answers. The approach question allows them to compare their personal thoughts and feelings with what they later discover in Scripture.

**Question 2.** Because the passage is long and rich, your job as leader is both to be aware of time and to lead the group into fuller discussion where needs present themselves. Feel free to use follow-up questions to enhance discussion in needed areas.

"Admiring gratitude shines through every line of this hymn to the God of all grace, for which the next psalm, 104, seems to have been written as a companion (to judge from its matching opening and close). Together the psalms praise God as Saviour and Creator, Father and Sustainer, 'merciful and mighty'. In the galaxy of the Psalter these are twin stars of the first magnitude.

"All God does stems from who he is (*name*) and what he is (*holy*): He never acts outside what he has revealed and what he is. . ." (Derek Kidner, *Psalms 73–150* [London: InterVarsity, 1975], 363–64).

**Question 3.** In order to get to the substance of this question, you need to discuss what each phrase means. For example, "What does it mean to redeem your life from the pit or to crown you with love and compassion?" or "What does it mean to satisfy your desires with good things so that your youth is renewed like the eagle's?"

"The blend of changeless fatherly care and endless sovereign rule is the distinctive stress of this psalm" (*The New Bible Commentary,* 552).

"It is more than eloquence that has shaped this stanza in the form of inward dialogue. It is not the only instance of a psalmist's rousing of himself to shake off apathy or gloom, using his mind and memory to kindle his emotions. And there is fuel enough in verses 2–5 for more than kindling" (Kidner, *Psalms 73–150,* 363–64).

**Question 4.** "The psalm opens (1–5) on a personal note: how these attributes of grace have acted in my life. . . .

"*Praise* is the distinctive word 'Bless'. When the Lord blesses us he reviews our needs and responds to them; when we bless the Lord, we review his excellencies and respond to them" (*The New Bible Commentary,* 552).

The beauty of Scripture is that it can meet us where we are. Lead the group in openly sharing their needs and how they are met by God's kindness. You may want to pray for each other at the end of the study based on the responses to this question.

**Question 5.** Be sure to explore both who God is and what he does. You will discover that what he does flows from who he is.

"No story surpasses the Exodus for a record of human unworthiness: of grace abounding and 'benefits forgot'. Its mention here (7) reminds us of the sullen ingratitude which God encounters in reply to the forgiving, healing and redeeming of which the opening verses sang.

"This poem 'pivots' on v 11 with its affirmation of overshadowing, over-mastering, (*great is* translated *flooded* in Gen. 7:24), 'ever-unchanging' *love*. It moves towards this central truth in matching steps: (I) 6 and 17–18 affirm the Lord's *righteousness*, i.e. is inflexible commitment to his own righteous nature and purposes: he never loves through any adjustment of his holiness or relaxation of his standards. His righteousness is the stamp of all his actions. To the human eye many wrongs go unrighted and oppressions unrelieved: v 6 says that the Lord sees to it that this is not so (Gen. 18:25); and motivated by his *love*, the Lord sees to it that right prevails for those who live obediently within his covenant (17–18).... 9–10 and 12–13 are the negative and positive sides of divine dealing with our sin" (*The New Bible Commentary*, 552–53).

"If immeasurable distances are one way of expressing immeasurable love and mercy (*cf.* Ephe. 3:18f.; Is. 55:6–9), the intimacy of a family is another.... But verse 14 adds that this father *knows* as deeply as He cares. *Cf.* NEB, 'For he knows how we are made'—and the *he* is empathic. He knows us even better than we know ourselves" (Kidner, *Psalms 73–150*, 363–64).

**Question 8.** The point of this question is not to get at particular sins but at our inability to believe that God forgives and forgets our sin when we confess and repent. Many people struggle with this and thus miss the joy and the freedom of living in his forgiveness. Part of the problem has to do with forgiving ourselves.

"East and west can never meet. This is a symbolic portrait of God's forgiveness—when he forgives our sin, he separates it from us and doesn't even remember it. We need never wallow in the forgiven past, for God forgives and forgets. We tend to dredge up the ugly past, but God will not do this for he has wiped our record clean. If we are to follow God, we must model his forgiveness. When we forgive another, we must also forget the sin. Otherwise, we have not truly forgiven" (*Life Application Bible* [Wheaton, Ill.: Tyndale, 1988], note on Psalm 103:12).

"Forgetting" the sins of others that we have forgiven does not mean a sudden loss of memory. Rather, we determine never to hold that offense against the person who is forgiven. We do not dwell on the offense. The literal forgiving will follow.

**Question 9.** "Grass and wild flowers, so brief in their glory, are a favourite theme, sometimes for comparison. . . . Our Lord gave a new turn to this analogy from nature, arguing from God's care for things as fragile as flowers to His far greater care for us" (Kidner, *Psalms 73–150, 366*).

*Study 2*

# SHOWING KINDNESS TO OTHERS

*Matthew 10:40–42; Mark 9:33–37*

**Purpose:** To realize that when we show kindness to the least of Christ's followers, we are being kind to Jesus and to his Father.

**Question 2.** "The person who relinquishes the right to his or her own life (10:38–39) becomes a representative of Jesus (10:40–42; compare 18:5; Mark 9:37; Luke 10:16, John 13:20), and one must receive a herald or ambassador in the same way one would receive *the one who sent* him (for the principle applied to the apostle, compare 2 Cor. 5:20–6:2, 11–13; 7:2–40). Some in Jesus' day seem to have advocated receiving the sages as God's representatives, but for Jesus it was those who became like children—the epitome of dependence and powerlessness in antiquity—who were his representatives (Matt. 10:42; 11:25; 18:5–6).

"As people treat God's prophet, so they treat the God who sent the prophet (1 Sam. 8:7). Matthew repeatedly emphasizes that disciples as Jesus' agents are his righteous ones and prophets, even greater than prophets of old (Matt. 511–12; 11:9; 13:17). Disciples were also *little ones* (10:42), the easily oppressed and powerless who could not or would not defend themselves, hence depended solely on God (18:3–6, 10; compare Mark 9:37; 10:14–15)" (Craig S. Keener, *Matthew,* The IVP New Testament Commentary Series [Downers Grove, Ill.: InterVarsity, 1997], 211).

Whether we are receiving apostles or "little ones," we are, in fact, receiving Christ. The value he places on each of his followers obliterates class distinctions—at least as a motive for showing kindness (see also question 11).

**Question 4.** "Receiving Jesus' representatives with *a cup of water* (Matt. 10:42; Mark 9:41) probably refers to accepting into one's home missionaries who have abandoned their own homes and security to bring

Christ's message. A cup of cold water might have been all that a peasant could offer, but hospitality given in faith to a prophet who requested it would be rewarded (Keener, *Matthew,* 211).

**Question 5.** In an essay entitled "The Weight of Glory," C. S. Lewis suggests that our "reward" may, in fact, be that perfect moment of praise when the Lord says to us, "Well done, good and faithful servant!"

"To *give a cup of cold water* is basic eastern hospitality and needs no *reward;* but God's grace goes beyond our deserving" (*The New Bible Commentary,* 918).

Some members of the group may not be motivated by the promise of rewards. You might point out, however, that rewards provided a strong motivation for many of the biblical writers (see, for example, 1 Cor. 9:25–27; 2 Tim. 4:8; James 1:12; 1 Peter 5:4; Rev. 2:10).

**Question 6.** Although this is a speculative question, it is a very important one. The content of the disciples' argument and this question regarding the "why" of such an argument hits at the very core of our pride as human beings. Because the disciples' actions so closely resemble our own tendencies, the group may be reluctant to answer the question. This is a time for your leadership to set the pace for honesty.

We are dealing here with what a friend calls "God's upside-down laws." In other words, God's way of doing things is the opposite of what seems natural to us. For instance, our tendency is to push ahead to be first or at least to argue about who should be first. Jesus says, "If anyone wants to be first, he must be last and the servant of all."

"The Twelve still had to learn that part of the cost of the kingdom of God was ceasing to seek high places for themselves" (*The New Bible Commentary,* 965).

**Question 8.** "Servanthood and humility are the only paths to true Christian greatness, which is why Jesus took a child as an example here (36)" (*The New Bible Commentary,* 965).

According to Jesus, the question is not whether we have many servants, but whether we serve many. Likewise, the truly great are not on the top of the heap, but on the bottom. His perspective is the exact opposite of the world's.

**Question 11.** Too often the church follows the culture instead of having an impact on it. Like those around us, we often place a higher value on those who are successful, well-educated, wealthy, powerful, or attractive. What would happen if all Christians lived with Jesus' high value of human beings? He demonstrated his value of others, regardless of their status according to the world, when he stated that by welcoming them we are welcoming him. In making that statement, he obliterated all distinctions.

**Question 12.** Obviously our giving a cup of water does not need to be literal, though it certainly can be. But there are many types of needs and many distinctions made among people because of those needs. You may not be around someone who is deprived materially, but you may know someone who has other "unacceptable" needs. Think carefully about the relationships in your life and who needs special care from you.

*Study 3*

## KINDNESS ILLUSTRATED:
## BOAZ AND RUTH

*Ruth 2*

**Purpose:** To see a biblical example of kindness and to integrate kindness more into our lives and relationships.

**Question 2.** "Ruth, who knew nothing about Boaz, proposed to take advantage of the ancient law permitting the needy to glean in the fields at harvest time (cf. Lev. 19:9, 23:22, Deut. 24:19), so sparing Naomi the toil and humiliation such work involved" (*The New Bible Commentary: Revised,* 280).

Ruth also demonstrates her commitment by working hard and faithfully (v. 7), by admitting her need and preparing for Naomi's future wellbeing as well as her own (v. 13), by sharing all she had with her mother-in-law (v. 18), by sharing herself openly (vv. 19–21), and by following Naomi's advice (v. 23).

**Question 3.** "Ruth and Naomi's return to Bethlehem was certainly part of God's plan, for in this town King David would be born (1 Sam. 16:1) and, as predicted by the prophet Micah (Micah 5:2), Jesus would also be born there. This move, then, was more than merely convenient for Ruth and Naomi; it led to the fulfillment of the Scriptures" (*Life Application Bible,* note on Ruth 1:22).

"So Ruth went to the field and gleaned after the reapers. Slotki understands *she went and came* (AV RV) to mean 'She repeated the act of going out and coming back home again so as to familiarize herself with the bewildering network of country lanes, while at the same time making the acquaintance of decent people to whom she could safely attach herself.' But this seems to be reading a lot into the expression.

*Her hap was* (AV RV) is the translation of an expression which makes it clear that Ruth did not understand the full significance of what she was doing. She did not know the people, nor did she know the owners of the land. She came to the field and, apparently by chance, worked in a particular section of the field, the section which belonged to Boaz. Almost exactly the same expression is found in Ecclesiastes 2:14f. ('one event happeneth' to all men) and no where else in the Old Testament. It points to the truth that men do not control events, but that the hand of God is behind them as He works His purpose out. It was the fact that she came to this field and no other that was to lead to her acquaintance with Boaz and subsequent marriage with all that it involved (including, for example, the fact that it led up to the birth of David). Our author thinks of God as being in all of this. The Hebrew refers to 'the piece of the field belonging to Boaz' and not 'a part of the field of Boaz.' This probably means 'that part of the common field which belonged to Boaz.' It is said that grain fields were not divided from one another by a fence or hedge, but that the boundary was simply indicated by stones. Alternatively, the field-portion of Boaz might mean 'the fields belonging to Boaz.' Our author repeats the information that Boaz was from Elimelech's clan. The hand of God is over Ruth's action, and he does not want us to miss this" (Arthur E. Cundall and Leon Morris, *Judges and Ruth,* Tyndale Old Testament Commentaries [Downers Grove, Ill.: InterVarsity, 1968], 270–71).

**Question 4.** Boaz is an amazing and godly man. Look closely at who he is and what he is like. Consider what difference his relationship with God makes in his life and relationships.

"Boaz may have been a warrior, for these were troubled times and any man might have to fight. But in this book he appears rather as a solid citizen, a man of influence and integrity in the community and it is likely that this is what the term denotes here. Some suggest 'a powerful landowner.' The word rendered 'valour' is used of general moral worth in 3:11 and something of this may be implied here. The name *Boaz* is found again as the name of one of the pillars in Solomon's Temple. . . . Its meaning is not certain, but it may connect with the idea of quickness or of strength. . . .

"Ruth suggested that she *glean ears* after one whith whom she should find favour (Berleley, *someone who is **kind** to me*). . . .

"Boaz had heard of Ruth's kindness to Naomi, and when he found her gleaning in his part of the fields he took steps to see that she should work unmolested" (Cundall and Morris, *Judges and Ruth,* 269, 271).

**Questions 5–6.** "In the case of Ruth, who had no brother-in-law, a more distant relative was supposed to marry her. When the O.T. asserted that Yahweh was Israel's *Go'el* it underlined His covenant promise, by which Israel became His own possession (Ex. 19:5). He dwelt among His people (Ex. 25:8) and was their divine Kinsman, ready to deliver and protect them. The special contribution of this book is to make clear that the *go'el* alone possessed the right to redeem, and yet was under no obligation to do so. The willing, generous response of Boaz was, in a very small way, a foreshadowing of the great *Go'el,* who was to descend from him" (*The New Bible Commentary: Revised,* 278).

"Instead of being regarded with suspicion Ruth was accepted. She took nothing for granted but by bowing low indicated how grateful she was. Why should this farmer be so kind to her? The answer was that her reputation had gone ahead of her. The people of Bethlehem recognized goodness in action and approved of Ruth's courage in accompanying Naomi. With *May the Lord repay you* Boaz was expressing more than a pious wish. Aware of Ruth's self-sacrifice Boaz wanted her to be *richly rewarded* so that her faith would be strengthened by seeing all her needs met. Such was the promise to those who took God at his word (Deut. 5:10). God's people loved to liken God's protecting care to that of a bird spreading its wings over its chicks. Jesus' use of the same metaphor has reinforced its message (Matt. 23:37)" (*New Bible Commentary,* 291).

**Question 10.** "Naomi's delighted exclamation conveys her wonder at the Lord's over-ruling in leading Ruth to the field of Boaz. When she explains that he is one of their nearest kin, she uses the word *go'el;* already she foresees that the Lord may be permitting her to make some approach to him" (*The New Bible Commentary: Revised,* 281).

"Naomi proceeds to pronounce a blessing on the man who noticed Ruth (the verb is that used in 2:10). From this it seems that the result of

Ruth's gleaning was rather more than might have been expected. Naomi deduces that some special favour has been shown Ruth, and she looks for the source. Ruth replies that the name of the man is Boaz. . . .

"This news causes Naomi to break out in praise of God. She first speaks a blessing for Boaz, thus recognizing his kindness. But the bulk of her exclamation is concerned with rejoicing in God. . . . The whole drift of the passage shows that Naomi is thinking of God. He has not ceased His loving-kindness (the word that is used is 1:8; it denotes both kindness and faithfulness) and she makes specific mention of the dead as well as the living (though *living* refers to Ruth and Naomi the form of the word is masculine; cf. 1:8, where see note). There is a strong sense of family, so that any kindness that God might show to Ruth and Naomi is a kindness to their dead relatives as well as to themselves. Then Naomi goes on to tell Ruth the reason for her expression of pleasure. Boaz is a relative. The use of this term plus the reference to *the dead* may indicate that already Naomi had in mind the way events were to turn out. . . .

"The list of blessings had not yet been completed, for in addition to what had been mentioned there was the further point that Boaz had told her to stay by his servants until the harvest was done" (Cundall and Morris, *Judges and Ruth,* 280–281).

**Question 11.** "It follows that those who have experienced the Lord's *hesed* should be transformed by it, and so show this quality of love to others. Both Naomi and Boaz do so, but it is Ruth the Moabitess who is said to have shown *hesed* (3:10), where Boaz has particularly in mind moral uprightness, as well as selfless love and loyalty (2:11)" (*The New Bible Commentary: Revised,* 279).

"Ruth showed great kindness to Naomi. In turn, Boaz showed kindness to Ruth—a despised Moabite woman with no money. God showed his kindness to Ruth, Naomi and Boaz by bringing them together for his purposes" (*Life Application Bible,* introduction to Ruth, "Megathemes").

*Study 4*

# FULFILLING THE LAW OF CHRIST

*Galatians 6:1–10*

**Purpose:** To understand what it means to fulfill the law of Christ by carrying each other's burdens.

**Question 2.** "Paul's list of responsibilities in this section shows how those who are truly led by the Spirit can bring healing and unity in their divided churches. The responsibilities include both the believers' corporate responsibilities to one another and the individual believers' personal accountability before God. Our public care for one another must be matched by integrity in our private walk before God.

"The first responsibility of those who are spiritual is the restoration of one who has sinned. Paul's conditional clause, *if someone is caught in a sin,* is framed in such a way as to point to the high probability that members of the church will sin. . . . Paul is more concerned about the manner in which sinners in the church are treated than in the sin itself.

"Moral failure in the church should not be a surprise, nor should it be considered fatal to the life of the church. What is important is the church's response when such failure occurs. The church may respond with harsh condemnation under the law. That response will crush the sinner and divide the church. . . . But Paul wants to show that the occasion of sin is the opportunity for Spirit-led people to display the fruit of the Spirit in order to bring healing to the sinner and unity in the church.

"The exact methods of restoration are not described by Paul. They will vary according to the individual circumstances. But Paul does specify the manner of restoration: *restore him gently.* Literally, he says, restore 'in the spirit of gentleness'. . . .

"Gentleness is not only consideration of the needs of others but also humility in recognition of one's own needs before God. So Paul moves from his command for restoration in the plural form, addressed to all, to a command for self-examination in the singular form, addressed to each individual. Corporate responsibility must be undergirded by the personal integrity of each individual before God" (G. Walter Hanson, *Galatians,* The IVP New Testament Commentary Series [Downers Grove, Ill.: 1994], 184–86.

Help the group to relate this passage to themselves and their church by seriously discussing how they would feel (or for some it might be "how they did feel") if caught in sin by their church. The responses may vary depending on the kind of church community they are in or how they perceive it to be.

There may be some discussion on the lack of church discipline today. Don't let this become a tangent and take you away from the study. However, some discussion could be useful on what might be done so that spiritual discipline could take place in the church.

**Question 3.** "In order to bring healing to the sinner, we must have a compassionate view of the one who has sinned. . .

"Gentleness is not weakness; it is great strength under control. When gentle Christians see someone caught in a sin, they do not react with violent emotions or with arrogance. . . . The will of the gentle person is devoted to loving the sinner all the way to total recovery. Only the Holy Spirit can empower a person to respond in such a 'spirit of gentleness'" (Hansen, *Galatians,* 184–85).

"Paul defines the kind of mutual support and correction we should provide for each other: '*restore him in the spirit of gentleness.*' Remember, *gentleness* is a fruit of the Spirit. Our supporting, correcting, guiding and restoring activity is in the Spirit of Christ, who is gentle and calls us to gentleness. We handle each person with the kind of gentle care with which we would handle a piece of precious fragile crystal. We seek to be sensitive to the brittleness of persons, to their high emotional pain threshold. We are firm, seeking never to fall in the ditch ourselves in order to help the sinner; but we are gentle, recognizing that the stakes are high— in fact, eternal. We don't burst down doors to make our case. We respect privacy and dignity and self-esteem. We know that what is worthwhile is not accomplished by mere renunciation and rebuke. Our duty is not to condemn but to restore" (Maxie D. Dunnam, *Galatians, Ephesians, Philippians, Colossians, Philemon,* The Communicator's Commentary [Waco, Tex.: Word Books, 1982], 127).

**Question 5.** "No one should ever think he or she is totally independent and doesn't need help from others, and no one should feel excused from the task of helping. The body of Christ—the universal church—functions only when the members work together for the common good. Is there someone near you who needs help in a task of daily living? Is there a Christian brother or sister who needs correction or encouragement? Humbly and gently reach out to that person (John 13:34, 35). Any who feel they are too busy to help others take their work far too seriously" (*Life Application Bible,* note on Gal. 6:1–3).

Being doers of the Word is vital. Help the group be concrete and practical in living out the fruit of kindness.

**Question 6.** "The 'law of Christ' is to love one another as He loves us; that was the new commandment which He gave (Jn. 13:34; 15:12). So, as Paul has already stated in Galatians 5:14, to love our neighbour is to fulfill the law. It is very impressive that to 'love our neighbour', 'bear one another's burdens' and 'fulfill the law' are three equivalent expressions. It shows that to love one another as Christ loved us may lead us not to some heroic, spectacular deed of self-sacrifice, but to the much more mundane and unspectacular ministry of burden-bearing" (John R. W. Stott, *The Message of Galatians,* The Bible Speaks Today [Downers Grove, Ill.: Inter-Varsity, 1968], 138).

**Question 7.** "People make comparisons for many reasons. Some point out others' flaws in order to feel better about themselves. Others simply want reassurance that they are doing well. When you are tempted to compare, look at Jesus Christ. His example will inspire you to do your very best and his loving acceptance will comfort you when you fall short of your goals" (*Life Application Bible,* note on Gal. 6:4).

**Question 8.** "The alert man [person] gives attention to proper testing of his own work. Then his basis of self-congratulation will rest validly on his achievement, not on imagined superiority over the lapsed brother" (*The New Bible Commentary: Revised,* 1103).

"Someone in your group may wonder whether Paul's statement 'each one should carry his own load' (v. 5) contradicts his command to 'carry each other's burdens' (v. 2). Rather than giving your own answer to this question, ask that person (or the group) how he or she thinks the two statements can be reconciled. If they have difficulty answering this question, you might point out that there is a difference between the words 'carry each other's burdens' and 'carry his own load.' The former has in mind any oppressive difficulty that a person is facing. The latter stresses that we are each responsible to God for our own attitudes and actions" (Jack Kuhatschek, *Galatians: Why God Accepts Us,* A LifeGuide Bible Study [Downers Grove, Ill.: InterVarsity, 1986], 62).

**Question 9.** Receiving counsel from godly people is an important part of testing out our actions.

**Question 10.** Sharing "all good things" (v. 6) is certainly a call to financially support those who instruct us in the Word. There are, however, many other ways of applying this verse. For example, more and more Christian leaders are experiencing burnout. Though they are called by God to care for others and are equipped with special gifts to do this, they are human beings and need care and support. Help your group to come up with various ways to care for their leaders and to support them in more than financial matters.

**Question 11.** "*God is not mocked*—The Greek verb is, literally, to sneer with the nostrils drawn up in contempt" (Jamieson, Fausset, and Brown, *Commentary on the Whole Bible* [Grand Rapids, Mich.: Zondervan, 1976], 1276).

"As valid as may be the application by Christians generally of this verse to the unconverted, let us note that Paul applied it first to Christians. The general principle is clearly that unreceptiveness to gospel teaching and indulgence in carnal pursuits will bear its own fruit. What a man sows he will reap. From fleshly indulgence issues decay leading to destruction.

"On the contrary, to sow to the Spirit means devoting the energies of life to values of the Spirit of God revealed in and by Jesus Christ (cf. Rom.

6:19–23; 1 Tim. 6:12; Tit. 3:7). That which is of the Spirit yields life eternal (cf. 1 John 2:15–17). A man deceives only himself when he supposes that he can turn up his nose at God with impunity. No one can hood-wink God" (*The New Bible Commentary: Revised,* 1103).

*Study 5*

# REACHING OUT TO THE POOR AND NEEDY

*Proverbs 14:21, 31; 19:17*

**Purpose:** To understand why God wants us to reach out to the poor and needy.

This study is based on the assumption that your group does not fall under the category of "poor and needy" and that their basic material needs are met. If this is not the case with your group, or even a member within the group, you will need to adjust some of the questions and applications.

In any case, the topic of reaching out to the poor needs to be handled with great care. We need to avoid expressing a paternalistic attitude toward other human beings. Often Westerners have that kind of attitude toward those less fortunate than themselves.

Help your group to honestly address this issue. We are inclined to make excuses for not sharing our possessions rather than giving and sharing freely. We need to look seriously at what God expects and whether we are doing what he expects. As is demonstrated by this passage, God takes the poor very seriously.

**Question 2.** The proverbs use a device known as poetic parallelism, in which elements in the first line are restated and amplified in the second line. In Proverbs 14:21 our neighbors and the needy are the same group.

"The words *king, prince, nation, people, neighbour* and *friend* have made few if any appearances in the sayings so far; their appearance together in 19–21, 28 and 34–35 gives a community context to the regular concerns of the sayings on subjects such as prosperity. The way to use such prosperity is for the sake of one's neighbour in need (21) rather than to take the usual attitude towards the poor (20). Vs. 19 and 32 make that a matter of both morals and self-interest. Going beyond that, v 31 similarly adds religious motivation to it" (*The New Bible Commentary*, 597).

**Question 4.** To be "blessed" (v. 21) is to live under the smile of God. It is to live in harmony with God, with others, and with ourselves. It is to be at peace. It is knowing and resting in God's unconditional love. In what ways have members of your group experienced such blessings as a result of being kind to the needy?

**Question 5.** Please help your group discuss this question thoroughly. Modern western Christians can be unaware of the oppression of the poor in our society. Some examples of this oppression include: underfunded public education in poor urban areas, minorities being eyed with suspicion when in majority neighborhoods, a justice system that serves the wealthy, and churches that do not welcome the poor into their worship services.

**Questions 7–9.** These three questions demonstrate, among other things, how God identifies with the poor.

"It is not sufficient to avoid oppression of the poor: the good man gives active help, and since God identifies Himself with the helpless, such giving turns out in the end to be only a loan—to the Lord. cf. Matthew 25:34" (*The New Bible Commentary: Revised*, 564).

**Question 10.** "It promises faithful recompense, not necessarily one's money back!" (Derek Kidner, *Proverbs*, Tyndale Old Testament Commentaries [London: Tyndale Press, 1972], 134).

**Question 11.** It is clear from these passages that God holds the poor and needy in high esteem. He promises blessing for those who are kind to them. He considers it contempt against himself when they are oppressed. His identification with them is so strong that he feels honored if the poor receive kindness. He even considers it a personal loan when the poor receive kindness.

*Study 6*

# KINDNESS ILLUSTRATED:
# DAVID AND MEPHIBOSHETH

*2 Samuel 9*

**Purpose:** To understand how David's relationship with God and with Jonathan motivated him to show kindness to Mephibosheth. To seek to be motivated to show kindness to those in need because of our relationship with God.

**Question 2.** Allow a few minutes for discussion of David and Jonathan's relationship. If more information is needed, glance through the passages listed, which describe their relationship. It is a good idea for you to become familiar with these passages as you prepare to lead this discussion. This discussion will set the tone for the study. David's relationship with Jonathan is the basis for David's showing kindness to Mephibosheth. Their relationship is also a model of how our love and loyalty to God should affect our showing kindness to others in need.

**Question 3.** It was not a simple matter to find Mephibosheth; it took effort. David looked for ways to meet Mephibosheth's needs. He did not wait for the needs to come to him.

"On inquiry, Saul's land steward was found, who gave information that there still survived Mephibosheth, a son of Jonathan, who was five years old at his father's death, and whom David, then wandering in exile, had never seen. His lameness (ch. 4:4) had prevented him from taking any part in the public contests of the time. Besides, according to Oriental notions, the younger son of a crowned monarch has a preferable claim to the succession over the son of a mere heir-apparent; and hence his name was never heard of as the rival of his uncle Ishbosheth. His insignificance had led to his being lost sight of, and it was only through Ziba that David learned of his existence, and the retired life he passed with one of the great families in transjordanic Canaan who remained attached to the fallen dynasty" (*Commentary on the Whole Bible,* 234).

**Question 4.** David's kindness was an act of the will. He was motivated to show kindness to Mephibosheth because of his relationship with Mephibosheth's father, Jonathan, and because of the promise David made to him (1 Samuel 20:42). At their last meeting, when they knew that they would never see each other again, David swore to Jonathan that he would show kindness to Jonathan's family.

"After all he had suffered at the hands of Saul, it would have been understandable if David had conveniently forgotten his promise to Jonathan (I Sa. 20:14–15, 16, 42), especially in view of the fact that Jonathan had initiated the covenant agreement. But it was one of David's strengths that he did not forget what he had undertaken, even though many years had passed since that covenant had been made. The chapter provides an indication of the passing of time. . . . David had seen his enemies defeated, his throne secured, and his empire established. He was therefore in position to fulfil the obligation he had undertaken to show loyalty to Jonathan's descendents.

"David throws the net wider than his promises required, extending his generosity to any of Saul's surviving sons or grandsons, though his motive is clear: he is neither soft nor weak, but intends to show *kindness* (Heb *hesed*) *for Jonathan's sake,* for he remembered how much he owed to Jonathan" (Joyce Baldwin, *1 and 2 Samuel,* Tyndale Old Testament Commentaries [London: Intervarsity, 1988], 226).

**Question 5.** This discussion can take both positive and negative turns— relationships that lead us toward showing kindness and relationships that lead us away from showing kindness.

**Question 6.** Besides the fact that David had cause for a grudge against Saul's descendants, it was the common practice in those days to exterminate all members of the household of a previous dynasty so there was no possibility of their seeking the throne.

**Question 7.** "Mephibosheth was not only permitted life and property, he was given an honoured place at court" (*The New Bible Commentary: Revised,* 306).

David's action was not just a token gesture; it was extravagant—again, symbolic of his love for Jonathan. David was all-encompassing in meeting Mephibosheth's spiritual, emotional, and physical needs.

*Spiritual:* David displayed God's kindness and represented God to Mephibosheth. Mephibosheth's experience of David's extravagant grace and love could have reminded him of his relationship with God.

*Emotional:* Mephibosheth felt lost, forgotten, unimportant: "What is your servant, that you should notice a dead dog like me?" (v. 8). David did not look down on him, but put him at ease, treated him with dignity, accepted him as one of his own.

David provided for the continuance of Saul's line in spite of Saul's hatred toward him. This was very significant in Israel. It was an awful thing to have your family name die out and be forgotten.

*Physical:* David provided food, shelter, and financial provision for the future. He saved Mephibosheth's life. He did not kill him even though the custom was to destroy the families of a previous dynasty to prevent any descendants from seeking the throne.

**Question 8.** "In this generosity David went beyond what his covenant with Jonathan required—it was, in fact, 'the kindness of God'" (*The New Bible Commentary: Revised,* 306).

"Mephibosheth was afraid to visit the king who was treating him like a prince. Although he felt unworthy, he did not refuse the gifts of the king. When God graciously offers us forgiveness of sins and a place in Heaven, we may feel unworthy, but we will receive these gifts just by accepting them. A reception even warmer than the one David gave Mephibosheth is waiting for all who are willing to receive God's gifts through trusting Jesus Christ, not because we deserve it, but because of God's promise" (*Life Application Bible,* note on 2 Sam. 9:5–6).

"The kindness of God (v. 3), on which David modelled his kindness, was not limited, but freely given to the undeserving as an act of free grace. Jonathan had given gracious help to David when he was driven from the king's table, and now David has been able to show kindness in return by giving to Jonathan's son security and honour. 'Thus the love between David and Jonathan attains a new stature'" (Baldwin, *1 and 2 Samuel,* 228).

**Question 9.** Sharing experiences will remind your group members of what it is like to receive God's kindness through another and how important it is. This will set the stage for discussing the importance of showing the fruit of kindness to others. Encourage all types of experiences—simple everyday needs being met as well as more dramatic ones.

**Question 10.** At the very core of our showing kindness to others is our love and loyalty to God, even as David's deep love for Jonathan motivated him to be kind to Mephibosheth.

# BE SURE TO CHECK THESE OTHER GREAT
# BIBLE STUDY SERIES GUIDES!

## New Community:
This series creates an opportunity for a small group to study the Bible in-depth, as it builds community. Each study probes Scripture in a way that strengthens bonds and relationships.

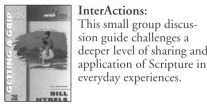

## Tough Questions:
This set of guides creates a nonthreatening opportunity to examine the difficult and challenging questions non-Christians ask about the Christian faith.

## Pursuing Spiritual Transformation:
These guides explore fresh, biblically based ways to think about and experience your life with God.

## InterActions:
This small group discussion guide challenges a deeper level of sharing and application of Scripture in everyday experiences.

## Women of Faith:
Designed especially for women to help them develop lives of friendship, joy, faith, and prayer, Women of Faith study guides bring laughter and encouragement to your interaction.

## Knowing God:
Develop intimacy with God by discovering his attributes, his love for his children, and his power to change lives.

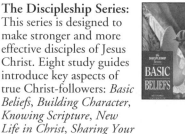

## The Discipleship Series:
This series is designed to make stronger and more effective disciples of Jesus Christ. Eight study guides introduce key aspects of true Christ-followers: *Basic Beliefs*, *Building Character*, *Knowing Scripture*, *New Life in Christ*, *Sharing Your Faith*, *Spiritual Disciplines*, and *Spiritual Warfare*.

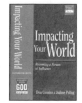

## Walking with God:
This best-selling 6-book series takes an in-depth look at your relationship with God and your action as a member of his kingdom. Two 500-page leader's guides, each supporting three study guides, ensure thoughtful, informative discussions.

## The Great Books of the Bible:
This study series leads you through a collection of eight foundational and favorite books of the Bible, including *Ephesians*, *James*, *John*, *Philippians*, *Proverbs*, *Psalms*, *Revelation*, and *Romans*.

## Living Encounters:
These guide you on a journey to faith at the cutting edge. Prepare to meet Jesus in ways that will expand your paradigm of Christianity, liberate your spiritual passion, and fill you with joy and spiritual vigor.

Visit www.BibleStudyGuides.com for more information.

# Leading Life-Changing Small Groups

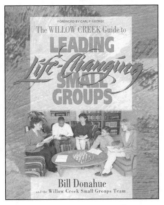

Bill Donahue / Willow Creek Resources
Foreword by Carl F. George

Like nothing else, small groups have the power to change lives. They're the ideal route to discipleship, a place where the rubber of biblical truth meets the road of human relations.

As vice president of small group ministries for the Willow Creek Association, Bill Donahue knows that small groups are key to building biblical community and thriving individuals. In *Leading Life-Changing Small Groups,* Donahue and his team share in-depth the practical insights that have made Willow Creek's small group ministry so incredibly effective.

The unique, ready-reference format of *Leading Life-Changing Small Groups* gives small group leaders, pastors, church leaders, educators, and counselors a commanding grasp of:

- Group formation and values
- Meeting preparation and participation
- Leadership requirements and responsibilities
- Discipleship within the group
- The philosophy and structure of small groups
- Leadership training
  . . . and much more

From an individual group to an entire small group ministry, *Leading Life-Changing Small Groups* gives you the comprehensive guidance you need to cultivate life-changing small groups . . . and growing, fruitful believers.

Softcover 0-310-20595-6

# Zondervan *Groupware*™

*Discover the most effective tools available for your teaching ministry*

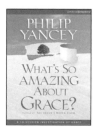 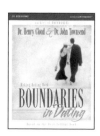  

Zondervan*Groupware* consists of curriculum packages developed with the assistance of experts and based on education research. Each resource simplifies the leader's role by giving them an easy to use Leader's Guide and bringing in experts and examples on brief video segments. Individual Participant's Guides complete everything you need to help your church members experience dynamic personal spiritual growth in a group setting of any size.

Zondervan*Groupware* delivers personal spiritual growth through:

- **Compelling biblical content**

- **Minimal preparation time** for both leader and participant

- **Proven learning techniques** using individual participant's guides and a variety of media

- **Meaningful interaction** in groups of any size, in any setting

- **Emphasis on life application**

Church leaders depend on **Zondervan*Groupware*** for the best and most accessible teaching material that emphasizes interaction and discussion within group learning situations. Whether a Sunday school class, midweek gathering, Bible study, or other small group setting, **Zondervan*Groupware*** offers video segments as catalysts to teaching, discussing, understanding, and applying biblical truth. **Zondervan*Groupware*** provides you with everything you need to effectively incite personal spiritual growth through interpersonal relationships.

Visit www.BibleStudyGuides.com for a complete list of
Zondervan*Groupware* products.

# The Fruit of the Spirit
BECOMING THE PERSON GOD WANTS YOU TO BE

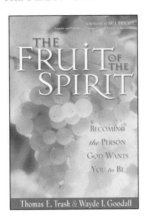

Thomas E. Trask and Wayde I. Goodall
Foreword by Bill Bright, Founder and President of
Campus Crusade for Christ International

Would you like true fulfillment in your life? Health in your relationships? Victory over anxiety and conflict? You can have them—if you let God's Spirit grow his fruit in your heart.

In *The Fruit of the Spirit,* Tom Trask and Wayde Goodall take you for a close look at love, joy, peace, patience, kindness, and the rest of the fruit of the Spirit. Here is a passionate and illuminating look at what happens to your thoughts, emotions, and actions when you live each day in intimate relationship with Jesus Christ. Drawing from the storehouse of God's Word, Trask and Goodall sow seeds of insight into your heart that both convict and encourage.

Your witness for Christ is as good as the fruit your relationship with him produces. *The Fruit of the Spirit* points you toward a lifestyle that makes the Gospel you proclaim attractive to others because they can see its results.

Softcover 0-310-22787-9

We want to hear from you. Please send your comments about this book to us in care of the address below. Thank you.

GRAND RAPIDS, MICHIGAN 49530

w w w . z o n d e r v a n . c o m